The Art of Persuasion

The Art of Persuasion

✦

A Practical Guide to Improving Your Convincing Power

Andrew K. Gulledge

iUniverse, Inc.
New York Lincoln Shanghai

The Art of Persuasion
A Practical Guide to Improving Your Convincing Power

iUniverse, Inc.

For information address:
iUniverse, Inc.
2021 Pine Lake Road, Suite 100
Lincoln, NE 68512
www.iuniverse.com

ISBN: 0-595-31080-X

Printed in the United States of America

To my dear wife and family

Contents

Preface

The purpose of this book is not to attempt to give a complete and otherwise exhaustive treatment on the subject of persuasion, convincing, and rhetoric. It is not written specifically for those involved in commercial endeavors, although its overarching principles certainly apply to this domain. Moreover, the aim of the present work is to suggest that active persuasion is commonplace in our day-to-day communications—that a recognition of this idea will have significant bearing on who we are as individuals and as societies. Realizing that most, if not all, of our social communications might be observed in terms of persuasion will invariably lead us to see the world from a quite different viewpoint. If the reader gains a higher level of awareness about the world and things, if this text provides useful insight into the human communicative process, if persuasion can be seen as neither inherently good nor bad, but as a fundamental factor of communication deserving our careful consideration, then the purpose and aim of this book will be reached as intended by

The Author

Unit 1: Introduction to Persuasion

1

Persuasion Defined

Persuasion is when you communicate information in such a way as to convince your listener(s) that what you say is veritable, acceptable, valid, and/or true. It is rhetoric. It is the convincing power. Persuasion is a fundamental component of human social interaction.

When your spouse convinces you that they are too tired and exhausted to take out the trash, for example, this is persuasion. When you convince them to take out the trash, this is also persuasion! When you talk your child into doing their homework, this is persuasion. When your child talks you into letting them put it off for a while, this is also persuasion! When a salesperson convinces you to buy their product, this is persuasion. When you reject the sales pitch, this is also persuasion—persuading them that you are not interested! Persuasion is very common in our everyday interactions.

2

Why Persuade?

Many people adopt a "live and let live" mentality in that they do not feel that we should actively persuade others according to our desires. They say that people should be able to do, think, and feel the way they want to. And they are absolutely right! Yet to think that people are utterly bereft of outer influence is asinine and irrational. People are clearly influenced in their choices. Why not cultivate this influence?

Let's say that you are running a little late for an appointment and you park next to a curb that has faded red paint on it. You wonder whether it is legal to park there because the paint is faded enough to make you question its utility. Yet because you are late, you park there anyway. You return to find a traffic official in front of your car, reading your license plate number, and writing you out a ticket. What do you do? Would you adopt a "live and let live" mentality under these circumstances? Or would you try to persuade the official that you are undeserving of a parking ticket?

Do you ever communicate anything to anybody? Do you ever have anything communicated to you? If so, then you can apply these principles of persuasion to your life. Yet when something is communicated to you, you have a choice of how to respond to that communication. You can accept it, reject it, or remain neutral. If you wish to relinquish your choice of how to respond, this is also possible. Therefore, whether you are the communicator or the one to whom something is communicated, knowing about persuasion will yield greater understanding in your social interactions.

Why persuade? We should persuade because whether or not we are aware of it, we will be persuading anyway! We might as well know what we are doing in the process of persuasion rather than taking a more ignorant approach. We should know about persuasion because whether we acknowledge it or not, we will invariably be persuaded time and time again in our lives.

We can persuade others to a number of things. We can persuade others to *do* something, to *think* something, or to *feel* something. We can persuade to understanding, to comprehension, and to conceptual integration. We can persuade others to adopt our system of values or beliefs. We can persuade to conversion or to apostasy. We can persuade knowingly or unknowingly. We can persuade others, and we can even persuade ourselves!

3

Communication as Persuasion

Persuasion is, to some degree, inevitable. What social interaction is wholly bereft of some form of persuasion? The entire human communicative process can be seen as entailing some form of persuasion. That is, by virtue of communicating with somebody, they are, on some level, expected to understand what is being said. If they do, then you have persuaded them to that understanding. Persuasion is inevitable in human social interaction.

When you say, *good morning* to somebody, what are you trying to communicate? To what are you trying to persuade your listener? Perhaps you wish to persuade your listener that the morning is, indeed, good. Perhaps you wish to persuade your listener that you are interested in having seen them. Or perhaps you simply wish to persuade your listener that you have at least a basic and rudimentary understanding of common courtesy. Maybe you say *good morning* in such a way as to persuade your listener that you are too busy and do not wish to be disturbed (with this message's commensurate nonverbal behavior/gestures)! There are limitless possibilities as to what a simple *good morning* can mean.

Silence can also be a form of persuasion. If somebody has wronged you and you respond to their *good morning* with silence, what are you telling them? What would it mean if you looked them in the eye while giving them your silence? You might wish to persuade this person that you are upset with them. You might want to persuade this person that you do not wish to talk to them. You might wish to persuade this person that they are not worth acknowledging! Therefore, responding to somebody's *good morning* with cold silence might be quite persuasive to these aims!

You may wish to communicate to a class that you are teaching about a particular topic of study. You would be persuading them to accept what you are teaching as being veritable and true. What good would a history teacher do in teaching about the Civil War if the students are not persuaded that the events related to the Civil War even occurred? What good would a math teacher do in teaching about *imaginary numbers* if the students are not persuaded to their utility and usefulness? What good would a biology teacher do if the students do not believe in the existence of cells, microorganisms, or ecological systems? In each of these circumstances, the operative persuasion is subtle and, in general, easily accepted. Yet certain other forms of persuasion are not as easily accepted.

4

Inherently Neutral

Persuasion is inherently neither good nor bad, even though it can be used for both good and bad purposes. Is television good or bad? What about the Internet? What about food? What about music, literature, or pharmaceuticals (i.e. drugs)? Some of these things can give us physical sustenance, vital information, and wholesome entertainment. They can also waste our time, engorge us, and lead to our degeneracy and destruction. They can bring us lifesaving medicine, nourishment, and information. They can also bring us devastation and disaster. On one hand, these factors can be a matter of preserving a life. On the other hand, they can be a matter of destroying one.

In like manner, *persuasion* is inherently neither good nor bad. It all depends on how it is used. Adolf Hitler used persuasion quite effectively resulting in the horrific devastation and great destruction known as the Holocaust. The American Founders, on the other hand, used it to establish the United States of America. Some radical religious cults have led to mass suicide by using persuasion. Other religious communities have used it to relieve suffering and benefit humankind all over the world. From a Christian perspective, Satan uses persuasion to tempt and seduce. Jesus uses it to uplift and ennoble. Persuasion, like many other things in this world, can be used for just, noble, and otherwise worthy causes. It might also be used for dark, benighted, and otherwise unworthy causes. It is our responsibility to utilize persuasion in a responsible and ethical manner, as will be discussed later.

5

Intentional Persuasion vs. Accidental Persuasion

Is persuasion always intentional? No. Persuasion can also be accidental. When parents have smoked their entire adult lives, what do the children learn in regards to smoking? If the children see the positive effects that smoking has had on their parents (e.g. perceived relaxation/temporarily reduced anxiety, weight loss, perceived social acceptance), and if they look up to their parents as exemplars, then perhaps they will be persuaded to smoke, rather than to not smoke. If, on the other hand, the children see the detriments that smoking has had on their parents, if they have learned to loathe smoking because they have had to live with it, then perhaps they will be persuaded not to smoke. Much of this persuasion is obviously dependent upon the child's perception and experience. Therefore, persuasion is not always intentional or "on purpose." It is often unintentional or accidental.

6

The Role of the Listener

Persuasion, as with communication in general, is a two-way process. There is, therefore, no "cookie-cutter" way of applying persuasion that will work in every situation. It is perhaps as dependent upon those who are persuaded (or not persuaded) as upon those who do the persuading. As with the tango, it takes two to persuade.

The listener plays a key role in the process of persuasion. It is the listener, not the persuader, who makes the true evaluation of the persuasion attempt. That is, successful persuasion will yield a different response in the listener than will unsuccessful persuasion. The decision (assuming an overt choice) ultimately lies with the listener, as does an *unconscious* acceptance or rejection.

Suppose you are trying to convince a group of coworkers to adopt a new administrative procedure. Let's say that you expertly use every persuasive technique that you can think of. In the end, the success of your persuasion attempt will be determined by the reaction(s) of your coworkers, not by you.

Avoid falling into the trap of underestimating the role of the listener in the persuasion process. Take comfort in knowing that the success or failure of your attempts to persuade might have little to do with your side of the equation. Your self-esteem might benefit from acknowledging this fact. Furthermore, you may erroneously choose to abandon a very successful persuasion technique on the basis of one failed attempt. Take the success or failure of your persuasion attempts into appropriate context.

7

Know Your Audience

Regardless of how you decide to use persuasion, you must know you audience. It will help you to gauge the propriety of logos, ethos, or pathos, and will guide your use of rhetorical questions or hypothetical situations. Understanding your audience will help you to be parsimonious, but not vague—clear, but not wordy. It will help you to know how abstract or concrete you should be. Knowing your audience is fundamental to persuading them.

You might try to use logos with somebody who values logic, and pathos with somebody who values an appeal to emotion. You might refer to something or someone that is an authority figure in the eyes of your audience. In using rhetorical questions and hypothetical situations, you can have an idea as to how your audience will respond to your suggestions. You can know your audience's level of sophistication in a certain area, and thus know how much explanation is needed. The better you know your audience, the better you will know how to persuade them.

8

The Irrelevance of Truth

Perception is more important than truth in the process of persuasion. For example, different members of an audience to a debate of presidential candidates might plausibly be persuaded to different positions. The content of the presentations might be the same for everybody present, yet there will be a number of ways in which those presentations are *perceived*.

Perhaps a Democratic candidate is talking about a welfare policy. The actual content of his discourse would be the same for everybody in the audience. The listeners, however, will each perceive this discourse in his/her own way. This variance in perception is fundamental to the listener's role in the persuasion process.

Carefully consider your audience's perceptions. As compared to perception, truth is irrelevant in persuasion. There is no such thing as truth in this sphere. You cannot assume that everybody sees things through the same lens. Everybody is entitled to perceive things (including persuasion attempts) however they wish to perceive them. Consider this as you attempt to persuade others.

Two people argue over which is better—pizza or spaghetti. Each tries to persuade the other to perceive things differently.

"Why is pizza better?" asks one.

"It just is," says the other.

This sense of something "just being" better than something else gives the false impression that there is some objective truth in the matter. The point is that there is no such thing as (objective) truth in these kinds of considerations. *There is no truth, only perception.*

If our two friends, arguing about pizza and spaghetti, were to realize that preference is a function of perception, not truth, their persuasion attempts would be free from such phrases as, "It just is," and other allusions to a "true" state of reality. Their argument might be something more like the following:

"You like pizza better than spaghetti?"

"Yeah."

"I really like pizza too. It's hot, tasty, and very satisfying. I really like pizza. But nothing quite has the fulfilling goodness of fresh spaghetti in a rich marinara, topped with grated Parmesan and meatballs.

"You're right. That experience is unique."

The one person has not only persuaded the other to see spaghetti as being desirable, but the entire subject matter of the argument might clearly shift. It may soon no longer be a question of which is better (assuming an objective reality or truth), but it becomes a question of what is good about each. Regardless of what the question has become, the first person led the other to admit that spaghetti is good. And this is a step in the right direction. The other person's *perceptions* about spaghetti are changing, but *truth* is irrelevant.

9

Choosing to be Persuaded

Free will is the notion that we have the ability to choose our own actions. It has also been called moral agency, free agency, and self-determination. *Determinism* is the notion that our actions are "chosen" for us by someone or something else. This is the idea that there are certain environmental "determinants" that dictate who we are and what we do. Do you believe that you have the freedom to choose your actions, thoughts, feelings, etc.? If so, then you might believe in free will. Do you believe that you are the product of your environment, your family of origin (i.e. the family in which you grew up), your surroundings, your cultural background, etc.? If so, then you might believe in determinism.

But do you have to believe in either one or the other? No! Some people would suggest that you have to be on either side of the fence. Yet I suggest that we can accept and believe in both free will *and* determinism. I believe that we have an inherent right to make choices, even though external forces influence those choices. I believe in both free will *and* determinism.

A man says, "I'm just an alcoholic. My parents were alcoholics. My grandparents were alcoholics. I just have the *alcoholic gene.*"

A friend replies, "Are you trying to say that you never chose to drink, not even the first time?"

"Well, yeah. I mean, I chose it and all, but I didn't ever *choose* to become an alcoholic."

"Could you choose to *not* be an alcoholic?"

This interaction reflects the free will versus determinism debate. The "alcoholic" man is opting for a deterministic standpoint—that he was somehow forced into his supposed alcoholism. His friend is adopting a free will stance—that he can choose to be an alcoholic or not. The man admits that he chose to drink the first time, but what influence must have his parents had in that choice?

People are influenced (determinism) in their choices (free will). And what are these influences? Do people influence other people? Of course! Can you influence others? Yes! This is rhetoric. This is persuasion.

Unit 2: Techniques of Persuasion

10

Logos

Logos refers to an appeal to logic. Through methods of rational deduction, you lead your listeners to accept your method or argument because it *makes sense*.

One basic example of proper logical form is that if *a* equals *b*, and *b* equals *c*, then, though deduction, *a* must equal *c*. If the first two statements are accurate, then the final statement must be true. The first two statements in this example are the *premises* of the argument. They are the stated facts upon which the argument is based. The *argument* itself is the final statement that you are making. You are *arguing* or suggesting that *a* equals *c*, based upon the two *premises* that *a* equals *b* and *b* equals *c*. This is logic.

One advantage of this method is that, when used properly, good logic is difficult to refute. It is hard to deny the accuracy of a statement that is founded on proper and mutually accepted premises. When you are thinking in your mind that *a* really does equal *b* and *b* really does equal *c*, then how can you deny the notion that *a* equals *c*? This is a solid argument!

For better or for worse, however, our world is not so clear-cut. When is something ever so simple as *a*, *b*, or *c*? Things are almost always more complex. (The simplistic explanation of *a*, *b*, and *c*, however, makes understanding these concepts much easier.) This is important because if I say that *a* equals *b*, when it actually does not, my whole argument breaks down. What if *a* sometimes equals *b*? Then I might get away with saying that it (always) equals *b* to the careless or misinformed listener. The astute listener will catch the flaw *before* considering the validity of the argument as a whole. Consider the validity of the argument's premises before considering the validity of the argument itself.

Arguments are often presented that are based upon poor premises. I might argue that all dogs are vicious because I have been bitten several times. Would you be convinced that *all* dogs are vicious based upon this argument? What are the argument's premises? One premise is that all dogs that bite are vicious. Is this true? This probably depends upon your definition of *vicious*, but almost any dog would bite under certain circumstances. Therefore this premise is probably not accurate. Just because a dog bites does not necessarily mean that it is vicious. A dog that bites a burglar, for example, might be called *heroic* rather than vicious!

Another premise is that several dogs have bitten me, which may or may not be true. Yet the argument states that *all* dogs are vicious, since *several* dogs have bitten me. This logic does not really make sense. It would be safe to say that *several* dogs are vicious, or *some* dogs are vicious. But to make the conceptual leap that *all* dogs are vicious based upon a few anecdotal examples is unreasonable. This is not a very persuasive argument.

A persuasive argument has solid premises and applies them appropriately. I may argue that one baseball player is better than another. If Player A has better statistical performance than Player B (the first premise), and we condition the "goodness" of a baseball player based upon those statistical data (the second premise), then who can deny that Player A is better than Player B (the argument)? One possible area of disagreement would be the second premise—that a player's "goodness" is defined by certain statistical criteria. Yet if there is an agreement as to these premises, the argument's validity will (logically) follow.

In actuality, it is quite easy to get somebody to respond to an argument without considering the premises or assumptions of that argument. A therapist says to her depressed client, "How is it that you have managed to stay afloat for all of these years?"

"Well, I just try to keep on going, no matter what happens."

The therapist got her client to respond to this question as if the assumptions inherent in the question were true—for example, the assumption that the client *had* stayed afloat for "all of these years." The client will be more apt to generate reasons why she has stayed afloat than to challenge the assumption that she *has* stayed afloat. *People are generally more apt to respond to a question than to challenge that question's assumptions and premises.*

One problem with logos, however, is that not all decisions are based upon logic. I was recently speaking with a man who could not understand the "logic" of using drugs. I asked him, "Is every decision that you make based solely upon logic?"

"Well, no."

"Is it wrong to base a decision on something other than logic? The decision to marry my wife was certainly based upon more than logic, even though it was, itself, logical."

"True."

"How would you like somebody to choose to marry you without any emotional involvement?"

"Not really."

11

Ethos

Ethos refers to an appeal to authority. A medical doctor's medical advice is generally more authoritative than a lawyer's medical advice. Yet a lawyer's legal advice is generally more authoritative than a medical doctor's legal advice. A family therapist's relationship advice is generally more authoritative than a hairdresser's relationship advice. Yet a hairdresser's fashion advice is generally more authoritative than a family therapist's fashion advice. Authority is persuasive.

Different things can be more authoritative to different people. For example, perhaps someone might consider their hairdresser's relationship advice as being *more* authoritative than their family therapist's advice! The authority of ethos, therefore, is *perceived*, not absolute.

I might perceive a basketball player's advice on buying shoes or drinking soda as being more authoritative than some no-name commercial actor. I might perceive scientific research as being more authoritative than anecdotal reports. I might perceive my parents' relationship advice as being more authoritative than relationship experts. Therefore, ethos is subject to the person(s) you are trying to persuade.

Think about what others consider as being authoritative. Perhaps the Pope's words would be more authoritative to a Catholic than to a Protestant. A conservative president's counsel would be more authoritative to a conservative than to a liberal. My parents' advice would be more authoritative to me than your parents' advice. Consider your audience's perspective.

Try to avoid falling into the pit of thinking that everybody thinks the same as you. As human beings, we tend to assume that everybody is like us. This is a fundamental principle of psychology. We think that others think the way we do because it makes sense to us. But take precaution to avoid making this fallible assumption. Avoid thinking that somebody else will automatically value the same things that you do, just because those things are important to you. Be careful to not make an appeal to authority that is only persuasive to you.

I often make the mistake of assuming that other people value scientific research in the same way that I do. It has come to my knowledge (rather painfully) that some people could care less about research. Yet I am still surprised when I try to use the ethos of scientific research with them to no avail. I might reference a certain scientific study, assuming that they will give it the same respect and reverence that I do. Being blind to these kinds of assumptions will significantly weaken your persuasion.

12

Pathos

Pathos refers to an appeal to emotion. It can be most persuasive. That is, an argument may not necessarily make rational sense (logos) or come from an authoritative source (ethos), but if it touches your emotions, it can be quite persuasive.

I once watched a television commercial about neutering/spaying your pets. With its sweet music and clips of little dogs and cats playing in their overcrowded animal shelter cages, I was soon in tears. My poor wife came into the room shortly thereafter and asked why I was crying. I was still too weak for words, but managed to blubber something about the commercial. Incidentally, we had our little cat neutered shortly thereafter. This advertisement had no real element of ethos or logos, but was most persuasive with its use of pathos.

As with ethos, the effectiveness of pathos is subject to those you are trying to persuade. Some people are hardly reactive to the use of pathos in persuasion. Others are almost completely dependent upon feeling as a basis for decision-making. One is not inherently better than the other, just different.

If you can use pathos effectively, you will be much better at persuading people. Try to notice what your audience values. If you were to try to touch a non-American audience with American patriotism, you may be missing the mark. But if you were trying to persuade a group of United States veterans by using American patriotism, you would probably have much more success. If you tried to use the pathos of music with a musician, you might be more successful than with a non-musician. If you tried to use the pathos of artistic expression with an art critic, you would likely have more success than with someone who does not appreciate art. Pay close attention to what your audience values.

13

The Rhetorical Question

A rhetorical question is a persuasive question. It is a question that you ask to make a point, rather than to receive a direct answer. Often two or more ideas are presented as being distinct from one another in such a way as to expect the listener to choose between them.

For example, I may ask, "How persuasive is an illogical argument?" Hopefully the point will be made without requiring an answer. The first idea in this rhetorical question is that an illogical argument is *not* persuasive. The implied second idea is that a logical argument *is* persuasive.

Now I could have simply said, "A logical argument is more persuasive than an illogical argument." Yet this is formatted as a *statement*. People are more apt to respond to *questions* than to *statements*. In the case of a rhetorical question, the response is mental, not verbal. Even though the listeners are not expected to respond explicitly to a rhetorical question, they are more likely to respond in their minds. This mental response is what distinguishes a rhetorical question from a simple statement.

I might declare, "A logical argument is more persuasive than an illogical argument."

You might say, "Okay."

But if I ask, "Honestly, how persuasive is an illogical argument?"

Your reply would more likely be, "An illogical argument is not very persuasive."

The difference between the two is the response in the listener. A rhetorical question elicits a mental response that the statement does not. This mental process of self-inquiry is what makes the rhetorical question persuasive.

If you are speaking with someone, you might want to give a little pause after asking a rhetorical question. A brief pause is all that is necessary. Pausing too long might actually generate a verbal response, or it might create the "uncomfortable silence" that we all hate. If you don't pause at all, however, you might not give your listener time to process the rhetorical question. And, as mentioned above, this mental process is what makes the rhetorical question so valuable.

14

The Hypothetical Situation

A hypothetical situation is often used for persuasion. It can employ logos, ethos, or pathos. A hypothetical situation is not necessarily real, but could be real. It is a situation in which you can manipulate the story, the characters, and the events in order to demonstrate a point. You engage your listeners to follow a line of logic that should lead them to accepting your position. Certain ideas are presented in such an order and configuration that will point towards the acceptance of your idea.

Consider the following example. Generally speaking, who would be more persuasive to you, somebody who is friendly or somebody who is unfriendly? A nit-picky listener might remark with a skeptical, "It depends." Another nitpick might come back with, "Well, I know some very persuasive jerks!" Yet the rest of us might conclude that, *generally speaking*, those who are friendly are more persuasive than are those who are unfriendly. In this example, I present a hypothetical "friendly person" and a hypothetical "unfriendly person." These two persons are not too difficult to imagine since most of us know both friendly and unfriendly people. The listener's imagination can then prove the point by itself.

Consider another example. Suppose you were walking down the street and met an axe-murderer. How persuasive would this axe-murderer be to you? This hypothetical situation is poor in that there is little likelihood of ever meeting an axe-murderer on the street. Even if it were probable, most people do not have a template in their minds for an axe-murderer's persuasiveness.

An improbable hypothetical situation, however, might be used with an appropriate disclosure. This instance might be if the use of conceptual extremes were necessary. For example, if we were to evaluate friendliness and persuasiveness, we might go to the extremes. We might consider a hypothetical "nicest person in the world" and a hypothetical "meanest person in the world." The first would probably be considered more persuasive than the second.

Avoid having your audience think of actual people, for whom they would already have attached meaning. This attached meaning might contaminate your "hypothetical" persons. Furthermore, if your audience is thinking of a real (or at least concrete) person, it is no longer hypothetical. Try to keep your hypothetical examples more conceptual than concrete. It is easier to have more control over your audience's thought process this way. Otherwise, your argument might quickly lose its persuasiveness.

Suppose you think of Adolf Hitler when I present a hypothetical "meanest person in the world." In this case, my persuasion would be rendered ineffective, since Hitler is known for his captivating persuasive ability. The conclusion is that mean people can be persuasive, and thus friendliness is not as related to persuasiveness as we would have otherwise thought. Thereby the "meanest person in the world" is no longer a hypothetical person, but a concrete figure to whom we have attached a considerable amount of meaning. Part of this meaning is due to Hitler's skills of persuasion. Therefore, try to avoid presenting hypothetical situations that might become concrete, and thus lose their hypothetical standing. You can easily lose control this way.

An effective hypothetical situation should present details in such a manner as to logically lead to the conclusion intended by the persuader. The story should be told in such a light as to make your position most reasonable and acceptable. Oftentimes, people will react differently to a proposal if presented in different contexts. For example, if I tell you that I am trying to persuade you to abandon your beliefs in order to adopt mine, your natural reaction will be to resist my attempts! Most people do not abandon their beliefs lightly, if at all. Yet if I present a hypothetical situation which logically points to the support of my position, then you might be more inclined to reconsider your beliefs.

Hypothetical situations usually have the advantage of objectivity. That is, you can often use a hypothetical situation when a more direct approach would be perceived as being threatening or attacking. The prophet Nathan in the Old Testament used this approach with King David. David sent a man to his death, so that he could marry his attractive wife (Bathsheba). Upon hearing this, Nathan used a hypothetical situation with David.

1. And the Lord sent Nathan unto David. And he came unto him, and said unto him, There were two men in one city; the one rich, and the other poor.

2. The rich man had exceeding many flocks and herds:

3. But the poor man had nothing, save one little ewe lamb, which he had bought and nourished up: and it grew up together with him, and with his children; it did eat of his own meat, and drank of his own cup, and lay in his bosom, and was unto him as a daughter.

4. And there came a traveler unto the rich man, and he spared to take of his own flock and of his own herd, to dress for the wayfaring man that was come unto him; but took the poor man's lamb, and dressed it for the man that was come to him.

5. And David's anger was greatly kindled against the man; and he said to Nathan, As the Lord liveth, the man that hath done this thing shall surely die:

6. And he shall restore the lamb fourfold, because he did this thing and, and because he had no pity.

7. And Nathan said to David, *Thou art the man* (2 Samuel 12:1-7, KJV, italics added).

A direct confrontation of David's wickedness would have not led to his indirect confession of guilt, as was the result of Nathan's clever hypothetical situation.

15

Take Sides With Them, Not Against Them

Take the other person's side. If you make them your opponent, then they will be less inclined to be persuaded by you—less inclined to accept your position. An opponent is more inclined to do battle. If they see you as being their partner, they will be more inclined to accept your persuasion. A partner is more inclined to collaborate.

Sometimes we can take a stance of opposition. If we posture our bodies as being face-to-face, this can be more confrontational and oppositional than a side-by-side stance. If we use "yeah, but" language, then we are setting up a pattern of opposition and debate. If we frequently disagree with their comments, then we are posturing ourselves as opponents, not partners.

You might say, "I like pizza more than spaghetti," and I might respond, "What's wrong with spaghetti?" Am I assuming the position of a partner or of an opponent? A partner would not immediately challenge the statement as would an opponent. If, on the other hand, I were to respond, "I love pizza," what stance am I taking? A partner is agreeable. An opponent is oppositional. This stance will have a profound effect upon the process of persuasion.

16

Process Over Content

Family scientists often emphasize process over content. That is, *what* is said is less important than *how* it is said. This gets back to the idea that truth is irrelevant in persuasion. Therefore, I might be stuck on the content of "spaghetti is better than pizza," but if I espouse the process of, "I am going to disagree with you," then I have already lost at persuading you. If I adopt the process of, "I am going to side with you since we are partners," then I have taken a stance more conducive to persuasion.

Unfortunately, most people are blind to seeing things in terms of process. They can only see in the black-and-white of content. Suppose your partner comes home from work and starts telling you about a disagreement they had with somebody. Many people would actually posture themselves against the partner, saying things like, "Well why were you late in the first place?" or, "Maybe you shouldn't have _____." The process is not, "I am here for you and I will take your side." It is, "I am against you and will be your opponent." The subject matter is irrelevant. The process of acceptance or rejection is what matters.

When persuading somebody, pay close attention to the process that takes place. Is this process more conducive to collaboration or to competition? Will this process lead to their being persuaded by you? For example, if you are trying to persuade somebody to your political beliefs, should you be open to listening to their own beliefs? If you talk over them, trying to give them reason after reason why your position is the best, what is the underlying process? Will this process tend to lead to collaboration or to competition? Are you making them your partner or your opponent? You may present the most eloquent and beautiful argument, but if the process of presenting the argument is poor (e.g. as with a one-sided harangue), then they will be less likely to be persuaded. *No amount of eloquence or logic can make up for a poor procedural posture.*

17

The Problem with Debating

Some people use debate as a means of persuasion. While this method can be very entertaining and educational, it rarely convinces the other person that you are right. In fact, it takes a very humble person to be convinced by his/her opponent in a typical debate. Also, debates may be persuasive to an objective, unbiased audience. Yet subjective and biased listeners might actually end up being as obstinate to change their opinion as the debating parties themselves.

The problem with debating is what happens both mentally and interpersonally to the participants. As human beings, we can be very selective about hearing only that which we want to hear, and seeing only that which we want to see. In a regular conversation, you may be very open to hearing and considering the other person's viewpoint. You can just listen to what they have to say without feeling pressured to agree or disagree with them. In a debate, however, your ears and mind become very selective. You listen only for things that you can refute and argue against. You look for inconsistencies in what the other person is saying. You try your hardest to disqualify the other person's statements. This is the inherent process of a debate. It is true whether or not the debate is public.

I might argue with you concerning religion. Supposing we are both Christian, we could "Bible-bash." I would pull out scriptures that will support my position and refute yours. You will cite passages that will make your position look good, and mine bad. The longer we continue in this manner, the more strongly each of us will feel about our own original positions. This process is inimical to persuasion.

When two people finish a debate, they often leave feeling more strongly about their own initial beliefs. They polarize. This is because of the interpersonal and mental process of debating—each person, battling to exalt him/herself and debase the other. As mentioned above, this format is fine in some circumstances, but too many people actually believe that this is an effective means for persuading somebody.

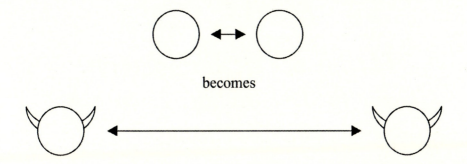

Figure 1: The Debate Phenomenon

Take Figure 1, for instance. In a debate, both people take a *competitive* posture, fighting against each other. What is the common result of a fight? The two parties polarize, moving further away from each other on the issue. Both tend to see each other in a negative light.

Too many couples try fruitlessly to debate with each other about their differences. They hold the erroneous belief that debating with somebody will actually lead to their accepting another position. But when you have them ready to do battle, the last thing they are going to do is surrender without a fight. That fight will lead them progressively away from accepting your position since they are engaged in a process that demands that they prove you wrong and themselves right. If you want somebody to come closer to you on a particular issue, it would be better for you to not saying anything at all than to debate. Debating is counterproductive to the goal of persuasion.

18

Playing the Devil's Advocate: Using the Debate Phenomenon to Your Advantage

Sometimes you can persuade quite effectively by playing the devil's advocate. This simply means that you take the position opposite to your own. You make this position sound so unacceptable as to virtually force the other person to refute it. In refuting the position opposite to your own, they are supporting your position. When you thus get the other person to argue on behalf of your own point, you use the process of debate to your advantage. You are getting them to polarize in your direction.

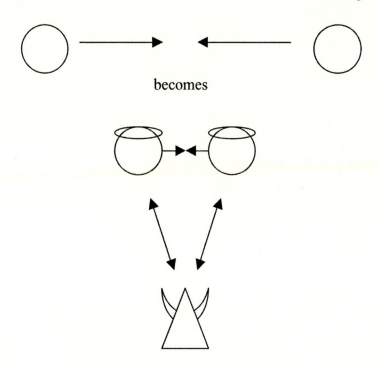

Figure 2: Playing the Devil's Advocate

Playing the devil's advocate is fundamentally *collaborative*. Debating is fundamentally *competitive.* Instead of fighting against an opponent, it is often more persuasive to align with an ally to combat a common enemy (such as the devil and his poor argument). Figure 2 shows how aligning with someone is easier if a third party is made out to be the "bad guy."

Playing the devil's advocate works with a wide array of people, but generally works the best with people who are overconfident in what they believe and hesitant to accept anybody else's viewpoint. These are the people that you often find gossiping about others. They are the people that pull you in close and tell you all about why "So-and-So" is wrong on a particular issue. When you play the devil's advocate, you create a hypothetical "So-and-So" and get the other person to disagree with "So-and-So's" position. When they realize that you agree with them completely in their opposition to "So-and-So's" ideas, you have indirectly (but quite successfully) persuaded them to your position!

"I don't need to learn another language. I'm just going to live in the U.S. for the rest of my life."

"Yeah! After all, everyone in this country speaks English, right?"

"Well, all except for the immigrants."

"Don't they learn English when they get here?"

"Yeah, right! Haven't you ever been to those towns where even the billboards are in another language?"

"Really?"

"It's something else."

"Sure, but why learn another language anyway?"

"Uh…"

Playing the devil's advocate is paradoxically subtle. The paradox is that you can actually announce (in some way or another) that you are being the devil's advocate. This lets everyone know that the argument you are making is not you own, but is a hypothetical posture—a rhetorical stance. This puts you in a very powerful position. The responsibility for your argument is shifted to an "evil" third party. It clearly lets you take some liberties that you could not otherwise take. The poorer you make your argument on behalf of the devil, the better off is your true argument. You can embellish your comments in ways to make them less and less acceptable. When your comments become less and less acceptable, the other person's argument becomes more and more acceptable. The trick is that the other person's argument is really your own! People are often all too willing to take sides on an issue, simply by virtue of your taking an unattractive alternate side.

On the other hand, you may want to let the other person think that the devil's position is your own, without telling them that you are just taking a stance. This might serve better to elicit a genuine debate response. But at the same time they might become frustrated and angered at you, rather than at your argument. They might distance themselves from you as in a debate. This distance might not only be in regards to an *issue*, but in regards to your *relationship* with that person. This can be dangerous. They might become so upset with you as to render any persuasion attempt unsuccessful. Use discretion as to whether or not you will tell them that you are playing the devil's advocate in making an argument.

It is also important to choose at what point you will tell the other person that you are simply playing the devil's advocate (given that you decide to tell them). If you tell them at the beginning, they may be less inclined to emotionally involve themselves in the pseudo-debate. If you let them think for a while that you are actually arguing you own position, they will become all the more fired up when you present a poor argument. They will be all the more inclined to tell you exactly what is wrong with your "position."

Yet when they are ripe in this emotional involvement, you can diffuse the situation by saying that you are just playing the devil's advocate, and that you could not agree with them more. When they realize that you were simply taking a rhetorical stance, the bad feelings that they had built up for you and your poor argument are suddenly transferred onto the hypothetical third party—the devil. At this point, you kindly agree with your partner and join in the crusade against the common enemy and his poor argument. Before you know it (and without explicitly stating it), you have persuaded the other person to your position.

Another purpose of playing the devil's advocate is not necessarily to get the other person to side with the opposite of your argument, but to stimulate the other person's argument through critique. That is, you might actually agree with the devil's position that you are taking. But in saying, "I'm just playing the devil's advocate here," you can challenge the other person's ideas with your gloves off, and not worry as much about the other person being offended. After all, you are just being the devil's advocate, not yourself.

Suppose you are discussing religion with somebody and you find inconsistencies in their argument. You might not want to confront them openly. Depending on your relationship with that person, an open confrontation might be awkward. But when you say the magic words, "Let me play the devil's advocate," the arena has suddenly shifted, and you can say what you really wanted to say. You can probe them in your questions to point out their inconsistencies. When these discrepancies are made manifest, your persuasion is often self-evident, not requiring any gloating or otherwise explicit declaration of victory. This process, however, is still oppositional, and should be used with discretion.

Another advantage of playing the devil's advocate is that you can be inconsistent in your positioning. You can take one stance one minute, and another stance another minute. It's almost as if you are being different devils. When you say, "So let's play the devil's advocate," everybody expects that you are going to argue contrary to what was just said previously, rather than being the same person throughout the duration of the argument.

19

Parsimony and Clarity

Be concise and to the point. Persuasion should be parsimonious and succinct. It should be substantive without superfluous words. A lack of parsimony is found in a watered-down presentation.

For example, if you present a hypothetical situation while giving too many unnecessary details, you might lose your audience. Have you ever tried to listen to someone tell a story in a roundabout way, without getting to the point? Few things are as frustrating as having to wade through superfluous and unnecessary detail in order to get the point. While it is important to be tactful and careful in persuading, avoid leaving your audience with too much "fluff." It will only detract from your persuasion.

Be clear and understandable. While it is important to be parsimonious, make sure to give your audience enough detail for them to understand and be persuaded. Too little detail can be as distracting as too much detail. There is a tender balance between the two extremes. You want to give enough detail, but not too much.

If, for example, I had explained parsimony by simply stating, "Be parsimonious," a few readers would have gotten the idea completely. Yet there are many readers who would not have understood the point at all! Thus I attempted to describe parsimony as parsimoniously and clearly as possible. I defined the term in a number of ways so as to make the concept understandable to as many readers as possible without belaboring the point. I also gave the simple (and parsimonious) example of poor story telling. When I felt that I had covered the issue with sufficient clarity, I promptly stopped.

20

Abstract or Concrete?

That which is abstract is more general and vague. That which is concrete is more specific and detailed. The continuum between the abstract and the concrete has been called the *ladder of abstractions*. As you move up the ladder things become more general and abstract. As you move down the ladder things become more specific and concrete. The concept of *Michelle* is more concrete than the concept of *wife*, which is more concrete than the concept of *woman*, which is more concrete than the concept of *person*. The concept, *Michelle*, is towards the bottom of the ladder of abstractions. The concept, *person*, is towards the top of the ladder of abstractions.

Being too abstract will often confuse your audience since speaking in vague generalities is very difficult to follow. Being too concrete will also confuse your audience by bogging them down with unnecessary details. It is a tender balance between being too abstract and being too concrete.

For instance, in describing the ladder of abstractions I give the concrete example of the concepts *Michelle*, *wife*, *woman*, and *person*. *Person* is the most abstract and *Michelle* is the most concrete. If I would have only given an abstract definition of abstract and concrete, then the concept would be much more difficult to understand. On the other hand, if I would have only given an example, without defining the concepts, they would have also been difficult to grasp. In giving both an abstract definition and a concrete example, I maximize the likelihood that the concepts will be understood.

Use discretion as to how you will approach your audience in terms of abstraction. They might be more apt to agree with you regarding a concrete idea than with an abstract generalization. On the other hand, they might be more apt to agree with you regarding an abstract concept than with a concrete notion. Try to get them to agree with you on either end of the ladder of abstractions.

For example, your audience might quickly agree that generosity is a desirable virtue. But they might not be so apt to agree to donate money to your cause. The concept of generosity is more abstract than a specific donation of money. You would be more likely to persuade them by working from top-down approach. You could slowly work your way down the ladder of abstractions from the broad concept of generosity to the concrete donation of money to your cause. Although this is not a foolproof method, it increases you chances of having successful persuasion.

It is also possible that a bottom-up approach would be desirable. Suppose you were teaching somebody about the importance of generosity. You might refer to an instance in which they had a successful experience with a specific generous act. Suppose they joined in a service project and felt good about doing so. You might then take them up the ladder of abstractions to persuade them that generosity is a desirable virtue.

Use discretion as to the level of abstraction you will employ in your persuasion.

21

Be Realistic

Be realistic. Don't think that you can ever persuade *everybody* to your point of view. This isn't reasonable. Would you wish somebody to hold this power over you? I have suggested above the importance of having the freedom to choose. I do not think that we should try to persuade people against their will. My model of persuasion is geared towards leading people to *choose* to accept what you are presenting for their acceptance. Therefore, do not be disappointed when you fail to persuade everybody to something. This is only natural! It is to be expected.

Being realistic also entails being able to see things from the other's perspective. If someone were trying to persuade *you* in the same manner that you are trying to persuade *them*, would you be convinced? Try to see things as if you were in the other's shoes. Try to place yourself in their situation and evaluate your methods of persuasion. This will help you to see how you are persuading from a more objective and external point of view. If and when possible, ask others to evaluate your methods of persuasion.

"How do you eat an elephant? One bite at a time!"

There are those who would try endlessly to persuade the Pope out of Catholicism, figuratively speaking. And bless their hearts for trying. But the zealous energy that you use towards a hopeless cause could well be expended towards a hopeful and realistic one. Why beat your head against a brick wall when there is so much else to do with your time, and your brains?

Persuasion often comes little by little. Don't expect too much in terms of persuasion or you will likely be disappointed. The level of disappointment is commensurate with the level of expectation. The more you expect in terms of persuasion, the easier it will be for you to be disappointed. If, on the other hand, you are expecting to persuade only little by little, then you won't be disappointed when you persuade little by little. Earth-shattering events of persuasion are few and far between. Let them come as a pleasant surprise when they do occur, but don't expect them to come all of the time.

22

Confident Modesty

A confident approach can get people to think, "This person must know what they are talking about." If you are too modest, people might not take your persuasion seriously. The most popular relationship experts, for example, seem to be those who are confident of their status as experts. Overconfidence, however, can be dangerous if it elicits too much criticism. It can quickly lead to a bombastic and presumptuous reputation.

A modest approach can be easier to accept than one that is overconfident. For example, if I were to say that there is nothing good about debating, then I would quickly elicit (valid) criticism. Furthermore, debating has a very appropriate place under certain circumstances. But the more modest approach of saying that debate is counterproductive *in certain situations* is easier to accept.

Sometimes very successful (and persuasive) people adopt an overconfident attitude. This overconfidence can generate controversy. This controversy can generate a measure of popularity and status. This popularity and status can generate a measure of ethos. This ethos can generate a measure of persuasiveness. The brazen overconfidence is not what is persuasive. The authority of their popularity, born in part by their audacity, is what makes these people persuasive.

Those of us who are family scientists often laugh when people consider talk radio or talk show personalities, for example, to be leading figures in the field. Their ethos as perceived relationship experts, however, is much greater in the minds of many laypersons than in the minds of marriage and family researchers—another reason why perspective is more important than truth.

23

Offer Something Better

A classic way of persuading people is to convince them that your method is superior. You offer something better in hopes that they will choose it. Since we are dealing with perspectives and perception, not truth and reality, this can be a tricky process. One thing you clearly want to avoid is insulting them. This will damage your relationship with them in such a way as to render your persuasion ineffective. This is related to how you should also avoid debating as a tool of persuasion. Remember, process over content.

The idea is that if you can genuinely convince them to see your method as being better than theirs, they will choose to change. There will be no arm-twisting, no begging. They will simply choose your method, perceiving it as the best choice. For example, if you learn a quicker and simpler way of navigating computer windows with shortcut keys, then you will most likely abandon the older and slower ways for the new. Indeed, I would not be able to hold you back from using the new method if you are convinced of its superiority.

24

Using Metaphors

For some reason, many people will believe your ideas if you can frame them using convincing metaphors. This is befuddling to me since a metaphor is nothing more than a figure of speech. Yet, somehow, people give credence to ideas that can be put into metaphors.

Some people might say that youth is like a rose in bloom; its beauty is short-lived before it withers and dies. Others might say that youth is like the dawn of a glorious day—a beautiful precursor to a stunning finale. Once again, truth is out the door; there is only perspective and perception.

The illusion of truth in metaphor is found in phraseologies such as, "It's *really* like this," or "No, that's not how it *really* is; it's more like this." People are thus pursuing truth in metaphor as they might chase an elusive butterfly. Take advantage of the fact that many people put astounding faith in the validity of an argument that can framed as a metaphor.

Unit 3: Theoretical Perspectives on Persuasion

25

Behaviorism, Perception, and Persuasion

Behaviorism[1] studies behavior from a scientific standpoint. One of its main branches is called *operant conditioning*. This suggests that reinforcement accelerates behavior, and punishment decelerates behavior.

If you are reinforced for going to work by being paid, the behavior (going to work) will be accelerated (you will go to work more) as reinforced by your being paid. If you are paid $100 per hour, you will probably go to work more than if you were paid only $10 per hour. The greater the reinforcement, the more frequent or intense the behavior will be.

If you are punished for putting your hand on a hot stove, the behavior (putting your hand on a hot stove) will be decelerated (you will be less likely to do it again) as punished by the pain you feel. The greater the punishment, the less frequent or intense the behavior will be.

Most things are both reinforcing and punishing, in varying degrees. For example, going to work may not be your favorite thing to do, but you keep going because the money is worth it. Working is thus more reinforcing than it is punishing. The benefits outweigh the costs. The moment work becomes more punishing than reinforcing, you will stop going—when the costs outweigh the benefits. Reinforcement and punishment are opposing forces that tug on each other. Whichever side's tug is greater is usually the one that wins in determining the behavior.

---

1.   Many sources expound on the works of Pavlov, Watson, Skinner, Tolman, Thorndike, Premack, and many others. The purpose of this treatise is not to give an exhaustive review of the literature regarding behaviorism. The ideas presented in this chapter regarding behaviorism are general principles of psychology, and are not the original contributions of the author.

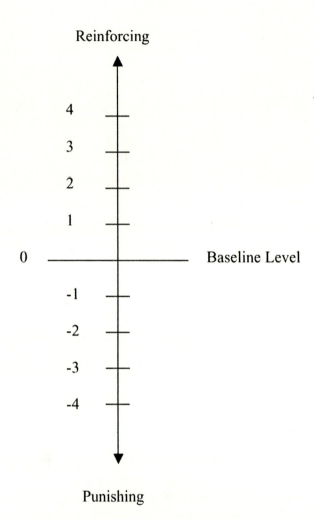

Figure 3: The Reinforcement/Punishment Continuum

To demonstrate this principle, see Figure 3. Zero represents the baseline level of functioning. Being above the baseline represents reinforcement in increasing increments. Being below the baseline represents punishment in increasing increments.

Let's say that going to work pays off such that it is at a reinforcement level of 3. Let's say that the work is also difficult such that it is at a punishment level of 1. Starting at the baseline level of functioning, you would go up the scale 3 points for the reinforcement level, and down the scale 1 point for the punishment level.

You would be left at 2 points above the baseline. This means that going to work will be more reinforcing than it is punishing (by 2 points).

Let's say that your job gets worse and worse, with your pay remaining the same. Let's say that your reinforcement level for work is still a 3, but the punishment level increases to a 4. Will you still go to work? Going up the scale 3 points, and down the scale 4 points, work will be more punishing than reinforcing (by 1 point). Being below the baseline level of functioning, you will stop going to work (or start working somewhere else).

If we were left to this theory alone, we might think that we have no freedom to choose our behavior. This is where cognition enters into the picture. Behaviorism does not determine behavior irrespective of perception. That is, the degree to which something is reinforcing or punishing is a matter of *perception*. Why don't you see many medical doctors working at fast-food restaurants? It is because they perceive this line of work as being far below their baseline level of functioning.

If you had no other means of making money, your paycheck might be worth putting up with a difficult job. For Person A, work might be at a reinforcement level of 3. But for Person B, the same job might be at a reinforcement level of 5. If Person B were to suddenly have an increased need for money, the job's reinforcement level might go up to 7. Suppose Person C came from a country undergoing extreme economic hardship. This person might view this same job at a reinforcement level of 9. *The level of reinforcement and punishment is subject to one's perception.*

If one's perception is so integral to guiding his/her behavior, then what if we could influence that perception? We might not be able to change people's circumstances, but in talking with them we can help to change their perception of those circumstances. We can change their perceived levels of reinforcement and punishment.

Suppose you are trying to persuade your son to do his homework. You could offer him money for achieving good grades. This would be changing his circumstances. You would be adding a measure of reinforcement that was not previously part of the equation.

Or perhaps you could talk with him about where good grades can lead—to a high quality course of study, a well paying job, and a deep sense of personal satisfaction that cannot be explained in words. If he can internalize this message, then his perceived level of reinforcement for doing his homework and getting good grades will become higher, even though his circumstances remain unchanged. If this level moves from below the baseline level to above it, then his behavior will change. He will choose do his homework. If doing homework remains below the baseline level in his perception, then he will not do his homework.

Behavior change occurs when the combined levels of reinforcement and punishment cross the baseline level of functioning. That is, the moment that something moves from being more punishing to more reinforcing (or vice versa) is the moment when behavior changes.

In general, the application of this theory to persuasion is simple. If you are trying to persuade somebody, make your method seem more reinforcing and less punishing. You might also try to make other methods seem less reinforcing and more punishing. You would try to propel your audience's perception of your method further up the reinforcement/punishment continuum, and other methods further down the continuum.

26

Addressing Your Weaknesses

Try not to be afraid of mentioning your method's weaknesses, especially if they are blatantly obvious. The point is that your audience might already know of them. If this is the case, then you can take the opportunity to address these weaknesses. For example, if I am trying to teach you a computer's keyboard shortcut keys, you might point out that they are sometimes hard to remember. I would agree with you. But I would suggest that the benefits outweigh the costs. For once you learn the shortcuts, they are shortcuts indeed.

When my method's weaknesses are on the table, I am in a position to show how they are inferior to the strengths. If someone points out how my method is punishing (on the reinforcement/punishment continuum, Figure 3), I can minimize the perceived magnitude of this punishment. In doing so, I can accentuate the pluses of my method as being superior to its drawbacks.

If I were to deny my method's weaknesses, then not only is this a process of rejection and antagonism, but I am setting up the conversation for debate. If I agree with you regarding my method's weaknesses, then there is no room for debate or antagonism, only agreeable collaboration. On the other hand, avoid sowing seeds of doubt where they do not already exist. Don't automatically spill the beans on your method's foibles. If your audience is already thinking positively about your persuasion, don't ruin it. Just be willing to discuss the weaknesses of your position if they arise.

27

Social Learning Theory and Persuasion

Social learning theory (an extension of *behaviorism*) deals with the idea that if you see someone being reinforced for a behavior, you will tend to infer that it will also be reinforcing to you; if you see someone being punished for a behavior, you will tend to infer that it will also be punishing to you.

If you see someone at work getting a raise for working harder, you will tend to work harder (inferring that you will also get a raise). On the other hand, if you see someone at work getting a raise for being dishonest in a certain way, you will tend to also be dishonest in that way.

This also works with punishment. If you see someone at work getting fired for being dishonest, you will most likely avoid being dishonest. If you see someone at work getting demoted for saying certain things to certain people, you will probably avoid saying those things to those people.

These influences are still only *tendencies* towards a particular course of behavior. The context of any behavior is more complex than can feasibly be discussed in an explanatory treatise. This makes precise prediction of behavior difficult. If you have firm values against being dishonest, perhaps no amount of reinforcement for dishonesty in your environment will lead you to be dishonest. No two people's contexts are the same.

28

Leading by Example

Demonstrating a method's reinforcing (or punishing) nature can be accomplished by either talking about it or by doing it. The latter approach is known as "leading by example." If someone perceives your course of behavior as being more reinforcing than another course of behavior, then they will be more likely to conform to your example. This is a positive example—a suggestion as to what one *should* do. If somebody perceives your course of behavior as being more punishing than another course of behavior, then they will be more likely to avoid conforming to your example. This is a negative example—a suggestion as to what one *should not* do.

If your system of moral beliefs is perceived by others as leading to a happier and more fulfilling life, then they will be more likely to be persuaded to your beliefs, by your example. If, on the other hand, your system of moral beliefs is perceived by others as leading to an unhappy and fruitless existence, then they will be more likely to avoid following in your footsteps.

Which of the two people would be more persuasive to you in adopting a workout program—an unhealthy, overweight couch potato or a slim, muscle-bound, and healthy individual? Assuming your goal is to have a physically healthy lifestyle, which of the two examples appears more reinforcing? Which of the two appears more punishing?

Commercial advertisers have utilized this principle in their marketing campaigns. Popular figures use their ethos to sell a product. "If she's doing it (and look at her!), then I want to do it, too!"

I once saw a humorous television commercial that demonstrated both positive and negative examples of deodorant users. The positive examples (using the marketed product) waved their arms about with confidence. The negative examples (using another product) held their arms pinned at their sides in shame and embarrassment. Positive and negative examples are a fundamental part of persuasion.

Unit 4: Conclusion

29

Responsible and Ethical Persuasion

Persuasion can be used for either good or bad purposes. It is inherently neutral. This is interesting in light of the fact that people are constantly (and often unknowingly) persuading people to one idea or another. Since persuasion is inevitable, how should we regulate our outward and inward persuasion?

My model of persuasion is geared around presenting information to somebody in such a way as to lead them to *choose for themselves* to adopt certain views. Anything that might be termed coercive or otherwise abusive does not fit within my idea of appropriate and/or responsible persuasion. *I consider abusive persuasion and coercion to be improper, irresponsible, and unethical.* I do not espouse or recommend this kind of persuasion.

One form of an improper use of persuasion deals with *dual relationships*. A dual relationship is when two or more people are associated with each other in more than one capacity. An example might be a next-door neighbor who is also your boss. If your next-door neighbor were your boss, would you be extra careful about keeping your lawn up? Would you make extra sure to silence your barking dog? Would you *like* living next-door to your boss? Probably not! You would be in a dual relationship. Your boss might clearly be able to "persuade" you to keep your lawn up or to silence your barking dog (or any number of other things) based upon the sole fact that they are your boss.

We cannot always control whether or not we will be in a dual relationship. What we *can* control, however, is whether or not we will exploit others with whom we have a dual relationship. If you did live next-door to your boss, for example, they should be very sensitive to not exploit you based upon this dual relationship. Your boss should be extra careful not to lead you to feel that you have to be an especially good neighbor just because they are also your boss.

Suffice it to say that any form of persuasion that is coercive, manipulative, violent, or abusive is unethical.

30

Mastering the Art of Persuasion

Persuasion is not some crude mechanical process. It is not a "cookie-cutter" formula to persuade everyone in every circumstance. It is not a foolproof method of "making" people believe the way you want them to believe. True persuasion is a highly developed skill. It is a talent. It is a gift. I do not foster the idea, incidentally, that persuasion is something that you either have or don't have—that you are either born with or without. I believe that although some people are more natural at persuasion than others, it is a skill that can be taught, honed, and eventually mastered.

I do not consider myself to be a master at persuasion. Yet I have been able to identify certain factors that have helped me to more effectively persuade others and to be more effectively persuaded myself. I wonder if there is anybody in this world that has truly mastered the art of persuasion! Yet since it is an art, its beauty lies within the eye of the beholder. And since it is an art, its effectiveness or ineffectiveness will not necessarily be judged in a concrete, right-or-wrong manner. Persuasion is therefore subject to each and every individual's own novelty, innovation, and creativity.

It is an art—the art of persuasion!

Additional Readings

I am not the world's leading expert on persuasion (and I would be wary of anyone who claims to be!). But here are some additional perspectives on persuasion.

—AKG

How to Win Friends and Influence People
  Dale Carnegie

Influence: The Psychology of Persuasion
  Robert B. Cialdini

Influence: Science and Practice
  Robert B. Cialdini

The Elements of Persuasion
  William A. Covino

The Persuasion Handbook: Developments in Theory and Practice
  James Price Dillard & Michael Pfau

Changing Minds: The Art and Science of Changing Our Own and Other People's Minds
  Howard Gardner

Persuasion, Social Influence, and Compliance Gaining
  Robert H. Gass & John S. Seiter

The Psychology of Persuasion: How to Persuade Others to Your Way of Thinking
  Kevin Hogan

Propaganda and Persuasion
    Garth S. Jowett & Victoria O'Donnell

The Power of Persuasion: How We're Bought and Sold
    Robert V. Levine

Artful Persuasion: How to Command Attention, Change Minds, and Influence People
    Harry A. Mills

Persuasion: Theory and Research
    Daniel J. O'Keefe

The Dynamics of Persuasion: Communication and Attitudes in the 21st Century
    Richard M. Perloff

Persuasion in Society
    Herbert W. Simons

Persuasive Communication
    James B. Stiff & Paul A. Mongeau

Seeking and Resisting Compliance: Why People Say What They Do When Trying to Influence Others
    Steven R. Wilson

Perspectives on Argument
    Nancy V. Wood

Persuasion and Influence in American Life
    Gary C. Woodard & Robert E. Denton Jr.

0-595-31080-X

Printed in the United States
24438LVS00001B/139-141

9 780595 310807